Fear Of Heights

The Ultimate Guide to Overcome Your Fear Of Heights

James Scott

Table of Contents

Introduction

Chapter 1. Comprehending Acrophobia

Chapter 2. Possible Causes and Triggers

Chapter 3. Types of Treatments

Chapter 4. Overcoming the Fear of Heights

Chapter 5. Check for Physiological causes

Chapter 6. Home Remedies

Conclusion

Introduction

I want to thank you and congratulate you for purchasing the book, *"Fear of Heights: The Ultimate Guide to overcome Your Fear Of Heights"*.

This book contains proven steps and strategies on how to overcome fear of heights.

More than any medical treatment and medications available, there are many things that an acrophobic can do to help ease the anxiety and agitation. Despite having acrophobia, life can still be lived happily. A person does not need to live a miserable life just because he has an acrophobia.

You can overcome acrophobia. It is a more than possible feat and is something that is within your reach, so long as you take the time for it. You just have to do some things and avoid doing some particular things in order to achieve your goal. Know what it takes to overcome your fears of heights. Read it from here. Act now and be free of the misery of carrying that fear with you.

You just have to know some things to enable you to be on the way to freedom, freedom from your fear. Whether such fear is caused by a past traumatic experience, is inborn or a product of some physiological defect, sufferers of acrophobia can do a lot of things to overcome the disorder. Know what it takes to get you on the way to overcoming your irrational fear of heights. Read it here and learn how to beat acrophobia.

Thanks again for purchasing this book. I hope you enjoy it!

© Copyright 2015 by James Scott - All rights reserved.

This document is geared towards providing exact and reliable information in regards to the topic and issue covered. The publication is sold with the idea that the publisher is not required to render accounting, officially permitted, or otherwise, qualified services. If advice is necessary, legal or professional, a practiced individual in the profession should be ordered.

- From a Declaration of Principles which was accepted and approved equally by a Committee of the American Bar Association and a Committee of Publishers and Associations.

In no way is it legal to reproduce, duplicate, or transmit any part of this document in either electronic means or in printed format. Recording of this publication is strictly prohibited and any storage of this document is not allowed unless with written permission from the publisher. All rights reserved.

The information provided herein is stated to be truthful and consistent, in that any liability, in terms of inattention or otherwise, by any usage or abuse of any policies, processes, or directions contained within is the solitary and utter responsibility of the recipient reader. Under no circumstances will any legal responsibility or blame be held against the publisher for any reparation, damages, or monetary loss due to the information herein, either directly or indirectly.

Respective authors own all copyrights not held by the publisher.

The information herein is offered for informational purposes solely, and is universal as so. The presentation of the information is without contract or any type of guarantee assurance.

The trademarks that are used are without any consent, and the publication of the trademark is without permission or backing by the trademark owner. All trademarks and brands within this book are for clarifying purposes only and are the owned by the owners themselves, not affiliated with this document.

Chapter 1. Comprehending Acrophobia

It is natural for people to feel some level of anxiety or fear when exposed to heights. This natural fear stems from the fear of falling or getting injured or even getting killed (worst-case scenario). However, when this "fear" is taken to extreme, such as getting very agitated or panicky especially when the person is not really in such a high place, it is not anymore natural or rational. This irrational fear of heights is popularly known as Acrophobia or Allodoxophobia or simply, the fear of heights.

Taken from the Greek words, *Akron* which means "summit" or "peak" and *Phobos*, which means "fear", Acrophobia can have such a great impact on the life of a person when left untreated. It can hinder them from performing even the simple act (for any able-bodied person) in going up a flight of stairs, stepping up on a ladder or chair. It can even endanger their safety especially in situations where quick response or action is required, since some sufferers are unable to move and seemed paralyzed with that irrational fear of falling. People with acrophobia suffer from panic attacks and extreme agitation when subjected to high places or structures.

Needless to say, people with acrophobia definitely do not indulge in mountain hiking or climbing. It would also be very difficult for them to become high-rise building glass cleaners or steeplejacks either. It has been said that about twice as many women suffers from acrophobia than men with about 2% – 5% of the general population suffering from it. The reason as to why women are much more affected by this disorder is yet to be explained by experts however.

Although, manifestation of Acrophobia differ from person to person, its usual sign include rapid breathing, nausea, sweating, shortness of breath, extreme feeling of agitation or dread. In extreme cases, sufferers can have panic attacks that they flung themselves off high places or are immobilized with intense fear, subjecting themselves to danger since they are unable to get themselves down safely.

Some often mistakenly label acrophobia as "vertigo". However, vertigo actually refers to the feeling of dizziness when in reality the person is not actually spinning or revolving. This sensation is prompted by looking up straight at a tall structure or high place or looking down from a high place. It is also triggered by almost any kind of movement or changes in visual perspective. Hence, vertigo can be caused by sitting down, standing up or walking, squatting down, looking out of the window of a moving vehicle or walking up and down a flight of stairs. It can be classified as height vertigo only when the dizziness or spinning sensation is caused by exposure to heights.

Chapter 2. Possible Causes and Triggers

A lot has been said and written as to the causes of Acrophobia. The most widely accepted theory however is that this fear of heights emanates from the natural fear of people of falling down, getting maimed or killed, born through exposure to heights.

Phobia for heights are triggered when such fear is taken to extreme through a distressing experience in the past either by the person themselves or witnessing others suffer from harrowing experiences involving heights. As a sort of protective mechanism, the unconscious mind conceives Acrophobia. This happens because at some point in the person's life, he may have suffered from an emotional trauma brought on by personal encounter with heights or by people close or known to him and was stifled in his subconscious. Thus, to protect the body from further emotional trauma the mind then creates Acrophobia, to avoid provoking the same intense fear when faced with heights.

The emotional trauma brought on by the fear of heights is not limited to personal experience or by the people close or known to the person. It can also be triggered by having watched a movie or a situation involving strangers which relates to heights or the fear of it, which left a distressing effect on the emotions of the person.

While the most accepted explanation of the cause of acrophobia is attributed to emotional traumatic experience or conditioning, recent studies suggest otherwise. Such studies revealed that the fear of heights along with the fear of loud noises, are just amongst the many inborn or non-associative fears. This means that Acrophobia is an advanced acclimatization to a world where drops or falls presents a major risk. The level of fear differs with those at the end of the line labeled as Acrophobic.

Researchers of this new explanation argue that the fear of heights is a distinctive nature found in humans as well as in many mammals. On site experiments involving visual cliffs proved that toddlers or even animals at varying age are loath to venture into a glass-floor with a view of fall space below it. This means that even infants and majority of mammals of any age, have that inborn instinct of being afraid of heights. This may probably be attributed to the inability of a person or mammal to maintain balance as height increases. As one go higher from the ground, one slowly loses visual perspective or cues which helps in maintaining balance.

When this happens, most normal people rely on the proprioceptive to maintain equilibrium. Acrophobic on the other hand, tends to over depend on visual cues. This may be caused by insufficient vestibular function or just a lack of strategy. It is important to point out however that locomotion in high places need more than the usual normal visual cues. Overloading in the visual cortex can happen which can result to confusion.

Experiments done by Scientist yielded several different sources of the irrational fear of heights. These are past traumatic experience involving heights or a fall, incapability of a person to perceive visual or vestibular cues, witnessing the reactions of people, especially by the parents or other elders in the family when in high places, the tendency to over rely on visual skills and the dysfunction which makes it hard for a person to maintain his balance, especially when in high places.

A normal person both employs his visual capacity as well as his vestibular system in maintaining his balance. On the other hand, people with Acrophobia, relies heavily on their visual skills, since they have a deficient vestibular system. The vestibular refers to the cues coming from the sensory system which is specifically devoted to the function of maintaining one's balance. It must be understood that a person needs to do a lot more visual processing to maintain his balance when he is high above the ground than when he is on the ground. When this happens, the vortex gets overloaded soon, which in turn leads the person to get confused and disoriented.

Sufferers experience acrophobia differently from each other. Its manifestations vary and in different degrees. Some people may experience it all the time while others may only feel the signs when exposed to certain stimuli or triggers. For instance a person can climb a flight of stairs without any agitation when he sees no indication or reference that he is already high above the ground such as when the inside an enclosed building or house. However, the moment the he sees the ground from high above or see some other reference to his location such as seeing another tall building across his location, he starts to manifest the symptoms of an acrophobic.

Chapter 3. Types of Treatments

People with Acrophobia need not get hopeless since it is a treatable condition. Treatments may include cognitive behavior therapy, reality therapy and anti-anxiety medication. Successful treatment is based on the premise that Acrophobia is a learned response to being subjected to a specific situation. These learned responses can range from disconcerting, inconvenient, humiliating and even devastating. However, these learned responses are distinctively prevailing. Just as a person learns a specific response, he can also unlearn it.

Center to the treatment is the therapist, who can help Acrophobic learn coping abilities to be able to manage their irrational fear of heights. Therapist helps people learn to comprehend and regulate thoughts as well as beliefs that aid in triggering the fears; learn and train themselves to acquire some particular social skills to enhance self-confidence and gradually applying them into real-life situations.

The approach wherein Acrophobic are urged to meet head-on and modify the particular attitude and beliefs that trigger the feelings of fear or anxiety, is called Cognitive behavior therapy. One component of this type of treatment is the utilization of desensitization technique which involves having the Acrophobic relax and visualize mechanisms of the phobia. This means working on the least fearful component to the most extreme fear. Situations involving exposure of the person to actual real-life phobias are also utilized in some cases, to overcome their fear of heights.

Medications for Anti-depression or anti-anxiety on the other hand do not really provide solution to the whole conundrum. However, they are sometimes used to help people better able to cope with their problems. When a person is less anxious or less depress, he is more able to deal with his problems squarely. Drugs such as anti-depressants, beta-blockers and tranquilizers are used to treat people suffering from a pounding heart.

Another type of treatment employed for people suffering from Acrophobia is hypnotherapy. This involves methodical desensitization and some other curative techniques done under hypnosis.

On top of all these identified treatment strategies and techniques, the one other thing that an Acrophobic can do to help himself is to undertake some actions that will help him overcome his fear of heights. After all, since the subconscious mind created the fear, the concerned person can do something to counter such creation. These self-help techniques however are only applicable for minor case of acrophobia. Those who are really on the extreme end of the line should not solely rely on one's self but should seek the help of experts.

Chapter 4. Overcoming the Fear of Heights

Acrophobia is the illogical fear of heights. Most of the time, such fears are baseless and are often caused by allowing negative thoughts to overcome the rational side of the person. Sufferers of this type of phobia manifest different symptoms and degrees of fear. People with minor acrophobia have the great probability of overcoming the fear by taking action on it, without needing to consult medical experts. However for those whose fear hinders their chances of work and from indulging in otherwise ordinary activities, they need to consult a Therapist first or an accredited medical practitioner on the field before embarking on any self-healing ventures.

To overcome the fear of heights, one must take certain steps to achieve such feat. This is only applicable however in cases where Acrophobia is only minor. A person can determine whether he is suffering from a minor case of Allodoxophobia or is near or at the end of the spectrum. When his fear of heights interferes with his normal daily routine, work or his time out with his friends and family, then that is already beyond the scope of a minor case of Acrophobia.

It is natural for a person to feel a little jittery or anxious when exposed to some degree of heights such as in a balcony of a high-rise building, on a roller coaster or even on a roof. However, if one feels panicky and over agitated when standing on a table or taking a flight of stairs, then it is time for a self-assessment on these matters.

CONFRONT YOUR FEAR

This method of overcoming the phobia is based on the premise that such particular fear is learned; hence it can also be UN-learn. However, in confronting one's fear, the person must take some steps towards the realization of this objective.

1. **Ascertain the triggers of your fear.** Before anybody can confront the particular fear that they are suffering

from, fear of heights in this case, one must first determine what really triggers such fear. Is it due to a past traumatic experience that left an indelible mark in the subconscious? Or is it because of something one had personally witnessed in the past? If your fear interferes with your work or with socializing with your family and friends, then one really needs to seek professional help. However, if you only feel a little agitated when standing on a second story balcony or before going on a ride in a roller coaster, then you probably don't need professional assistance. It is normal for people to feel some degree of fear of heights, considering that the fall (which might not possibly happen) can cause bodily harm and even death. One can only start to understand a phenomenon when you know what really causes or triggers it.

2. **Employ rationality**. Acrophobia is an irrational or extreme fear of heights. By definition, such fear is actually oftentimes baseless. If one only think

about it logically, such fear can be actually overcome. Entertaining irrational thoughts of the skyscraper you are on crumbling down or toppling down of the roller coaster you are riding on, you are on will only trigger baseless agitations and panic. After all, these structures are built to withstand almost anything and if ever they do topple or crash, that would be extremely unlikely. If your fear is minor, appealing to your logical side may help ease away your anxiety.

3. **Adopt relaxation techniques and strategies**. When gripped with fear, one thing that can help a person overcome such feeling is to learn to relax. In order to relax, one must utilize techniques and strategies since it can be hard to come to terms with your phobia when your body is paralyzed with fear. No matter how hard this may seem, one must at least try to learn to relax. You can start by taking deep breaths. Try to calm your mind by blocking out everything but the sound and sensation

of your breathing. Knowing how to meditate can help since one is already familiar with the techniques of achieving the state wherein one is totally oblivious to the surrounding but to the things you only want to focus on.

4. **Expose yourself to your fear gradually**. Sometimes, all you need to do to overcome your fear is to take that first step toward it. This may be a bit easier said than done. If you have an irrational fear of heights, especially in high-rise buildings or places, you might not be expected to visit the top floor of the World Trade Center or the Statue of Liberty anytime soon. However, you can start gradually by climbing the ladder up to your tree house or spending sundown at your second-story balcony. It can be very difficult to push yourself to do something which makes you agitated. Hence, you might need to create a situation wherein you will be obligated and forced to do it. This "situation" will serve to push you to doing something you might not normally do because of

your fear of heights. For instance, you might tell your mother or spouse that you will be in-charge with the housekeeping of the balcony area of your second story house. By committing to do such chore for the family and for voicing out your commitment, you have tied yourself into doing something which you might not undertake under any other circumstances.

However, you need to understand that if you are suffering from a severe case of Acrophobia, you should not even attempt confronting your fears since it might only aggravate it. Confronting it is only advisable if you are suffering from a minor case of Acrophobia. This advice is based on recent studies, which suggests that phobias or irrational fear of a specific "something" is not learned but is innate or inborn. Hence, confronting one's fears when it is inborn might not help at all in overcoming it but might only aggravate it.

5. **Adopt a mantra.** Telling yourself over and over again that you will be safe or no harm will befall on you while climbing a flight of stairs or standing in a balcony of a two-story house may help condition your mind to block out your fear. Since Acrophobia is created by the subconscious, one may counter-act it by redirecting your thoughts on the positive aspect by reciting some positive confidence-boosting mantra.

6. **Adopt a positive outlook.** An acrophobic mind is filled with negativity as far as his fear of heights is concerned. Feeling agitated and anxious that he might fall when it is impossible to happen in all probability is tantamount to entertaining negative thoughts. Since acrophobia is illogical, it is oftentimes baseless. Hence, if you learn to start a positive outlook, there is great probability that such gruesome yet baseless thoughts will have no more room in your mind. Of course, this is easier said than done. However, the benefits that the person will derive from

changing his outlook from that of being a negative thought-dweller to a positive thinker far outweigh the hard work it entails.

TREATMENT

If you have an extreme or illogical fear of heights which hinders you from interacting with your family and friends normally or from engaging in normal daily activities or attending to your work, then it's time for you to seek professional help. Treatment of phobias can include therapy as either a stand-alone treatment or it may be coupled with medications and some other form of medical treatment.

A. UNDERGO THERAPY

One form of overcoming your phobia when it goes beyond manageable is to seek professional help. This type of help comes in the form of therapy which is to be administered by an accredited and experienced therapist. There are various disciplines of psychotherapy which ranges from alternative methods to conventional psychoanalytic approach to existential. The goal of this treatment is to help sufferers slowly and safely diminish their fears while learning how to control their anxiety. There is actually no one "correct" or "right" method of therapy, hence Therapists utilize different methods of treatment. It is up to the person to choose which therapy suits and helps him best, towards overcoming his irrational fear of heights.

When seeking professional help however, you must ensure that you seek a therapist that has already been in the practice for some years or long enough to have gained patients who are well over their phobias and are already living happy, normal lives. With such patients, you can have someone to ask about their experience with the kind of therapy they have undertaken and whether they would recommend their therapist who practiced it. Beware of therapist whose work experience is limited to clinical studies and have never had any real experience with people who have real problems with Acrophobia.

It is also important that you seek the help of a therapist who is accredited. This means that the therapist you chose should be educated and certified on the field of Behavioral Science or related field thereof. Depending on the state you are in, your therapist may be required to possess a special license issued by a non-government agency before they are allowed to practice certain kinds of therapy. These matters are important since you might choose a therapist who will employ a method of therapy that will aggravate your condition, instead of helping you. Many reputable therapists utilize modern scientific techniques which have been published for review by their peers. It is better to bank on these types of therapist than to rely on those who tout of effective "alternative" therapeutic treatment or some other "homeopathic" methods of treatment.

B. MEET WITH YOUR THERAPIST REGULARLY

It is also important that you regularly meet with your therapist for the healing session as well as for the discussion of all aspects of your phobia. Going to your therapist only when you feel like it or when you are on the verge of one of your anxiety attacks would not help you. Before undergoing any therapy, you should first discuss your phobia with your therapist since the specific fear you might be suffering from might not be what you thought it is. One should realize that the fear of heights is different from the fear of flying or the fear of being in an enclosed place. It would greatly help your case if you are open and honest about your feelings and everything else that you think is associated with your fears. The more information you supply about your fears, the better your therapist can effectively treat you.

C. ALLOW YOURSELF TO BE EXPOSED GRADUALLY TO THE STIMULI OF YOUR FEARS

Therapist helps you lessen your fears and better control your agitation or anxiety. In order to achieve this, some therapist may employ the use of therapy which allows the patient to be gradually exposed to stimuli that trigger their fears. This process should be gradual since abrupt confrontation with one's fears might only aggravate the situation of the patient instead of helping him. For instance, the patient might first be made to imagine (while his eyes are closed) that he is standing on the edge of a rooftop of a very tall building. When the patient learns to manage this scenario without manifesting any symptoms associated with Acrophobia, the therapy session might move on to another exposure. The patient might be made to look on an image down below from atop a high place. When the patient can manage such situation, he will then be again exposed to another situation. Needless to say, each exposure will become more difficult or harder to help the patient overcome his fears in the process.

With the advent of computers, therapists can easily yet safely subject patients to different situations or stimulus through the use of virtual reality. Virtual reality in fact offers some exciting scenarios and possibilities that can possibly help Acrophobic patients deal with their fears better.

D. LEARN AND ADAPT STRATEGIES TO CONTROL YOUR ANXIETY

You will come to learn that therapist will not actually seek to help you totally remove your anxiety but aid you learn how to control it. As has been presented by new researchers, there is a great probability that extreme fear is not learn but is actually innate. In this light, we are still a long way from being able to effectively remove it from our system. What therapist can do however is to help patients learn techniques that enable them to effectively control their anxiety, thus helping them lead happier lives.

E. TAKE MEDICATIONS

No medicine that can effectively treat phobias has been formulated yet. However, some certain drugs help people with phobias better able to manage their anxiety. This does not mean that an Acrophobia should take just any medication to control his anxiety attacks. The prescription should come from an accredited doctor or medical practitioner is well-experienced on the field. If you happen to not know any professional of this type, you might consider going first to your "usual" doctor, who might be able to help you by referring you to the right practitioner.

You should remember however that medication alone will not solve your underlying problem with Acrophobia. However, the right prescription can help you deal with your life better since it will ease your agitations and make you relax much better. You will find yourself much more able to confront your fears when you are relaxed than when your body is taut with anxiety.

F. DO YOUR OWN RESEARCH ON ACROPHOBIA-RELATED MEDICATIONS

In this modern world where new inventions and breakthroughs in the field of medicine and science occur almost every minute of the day, it is understandable that your therapist may not know all about the medicines that are used to treat phobias. Hence, it would help your case if you conduct your own research and voice your queries or concerns or discoveries with your therapists about new medications in the market or even the ones prescribed by your doctor.

Some drugs may have ill-effects on you. Since these ill-effects are quite common, you as the user should need to assess whether continued use of such drugs far outweigh the ill-effects. To give you an overview of the more common drugs employed in the treatment of acrophobia, here is a short list of these drugs and its effects.

- Benzodiazepines – provides fast-acting, short relief for anxiety however it can be habit forming. It has a sedative effect which can also be addictive.

- Anti-depressants –these drugs which include Paxil, Effexor, Zoloft and other types of SSRIs/SNRIs typically act on and boost the levels of some specific neurotransmitters that regulate the mood of a person.

- Beta blockers – this medicine is effective in easing the physical manifestation of anxiety such as rapid heartbeat, shortness of breath and quivering. It works by suppressing the adrenaline.

Chapter 5. Check for Physiological causes

Some people may find themselves nowhere near the mark of being able to overcome their phobia even after intensive therapies and treatments. After rendering full cooperation and being in an open-honest communication with your therapy, you still find yourself embroiled in your fears every time you are exposed to certain stimulus. At this point, it might help you to consult other doctors who can assess and check your case for a possible case of a visual or vestibular ailment. The real cause of Acrophobia is not entirely explained, but some researchers suggested that one cause may be attributed to the way the body decipher spatial and visual stimuli from the eyes and the vestibular system.

In the case of an acrophobic person, he is unable to perceive correctly the visual and spatial hints, especially when in a high place where such accurate perception is greatly required. This misconception may lead sufferers to feel dizzy and confused, further leading them to miscalculate their actual distance from the ground. This "miscalculation" leads sufferers to irrationally feel anxious about falling, leading them further to feel agitated and even when they are not that high up from the ground or is in a considerably safe place or height.

When visual/vestibule perception impairment is diagnosed as the probable cause of the acrophobia, corrective measures can be undertaken to correct the disorder. In this case, acrophobia is not psychologically-caused but rather physiologically-caused thus should be treated as such. It is therefore important that such ailment should be diagnosed accurately so that it can be treated appropriately. That way, fears of heights can be addressed accurately.

It is exigent that the real cause of acrophobia be established at the outset so that the disorder can be treated accordingly. If acrophobia is to be attributed to something traumatic in the person's past, a hypnotherapy coupled with medication can treat such disorder perhaps. If the cause of the disorder is to be attributed to something innate or inborn, then it might take another method of treatment to cure it. On the other hand, if the acrophobia is to be attributed to a person's inability to perceive visual and vestibular cues, then hypnotherapy alone might not make any difference in the person's situation since the cause outlined this time is more of physiological, not psychological.

Nonetheless, keeping a positive attitude all throughout the ordeal will greatly help sufferers of acrophobia. It is perhaps the only thing that could keep the sufferer's sanity and composure intact, especially in times when the panic starts to set in.

Chapter 6. Home Remedies

Whether you are suffering from a minor or full-blown case of acrophobia, you can do something on your own at home to overcome such disorder, without aggravating the disorder.

1. Refrain from too-much caffeine.

As much as caffeine has its own health benefits, people suffering from any form of phobia should not indulge too much of it. Caffeine might energize you for a time but it will also make you high-strung and tense. Hence, cutting down on caffeine can help people with acrophobia less tense and more relaxed. Being relaxed will help sufferers better able to confront their fears, especially when the anxiety attacks sets in.

2. Adopt a healthy lifestyle

Adopting a healthy lifestyle means that you need to get appropriate sleep, exposure to sunlight and indulge in a regular exercise regimen. As much as normal people need to lead healthy lives, so much more for people suffering from irrational fear of "something", or of heights in this case. An unhealthy person who is stressed, unhealthy and who lack sleep won't be able to confront his fears with much confidence. Worse, he won't be able to manage situations which a healthy, relaxed acrophobic can readily accomplish. A person who exercises regularly, with adequate sleep will feel relaxed and refreshed, which will help him better able to manage his anxiety when faced with situations that stimulate his fears.

3. Cultivate a positive outlook

There is nothing much worse than harboring negativity in your life when you are suffering from a disorder such as acrophobia. Negative thoughts will aggravate the situation since the fear itself is often baseless and is the product of negative thoughts. By cultivating a positive outlook, you will be helping yourself negate the gripping sensation that usually took over when exposed to the stimuli. Positive thinking will help you feel relax and better able to handle situations which are normally stressful for an acrophobic.

4. Don't leave your fate to "natural" or "homeopathic" cures

Several homemade and herbal remedies have been claimed to effectively cure acrophobic or some other phobia. Nonetheless, these cures have remained to be officially proven by medical experts hence should not be totally relied upon to cure the disorder. Some may not make any difference upon taking but some other remedies may pose some danger to the person, in some cases. Hence, if you want to try these types of remedies, you should proceed with caution. It pays to be wary than sorry.

5. Don't try the "extreme"

One thing that might help an acrophobic overcome his disorder is to gradually expose himself to the stimuli that cause their fears. However this exposure or confrontation should not be brought to the extreme. One common theory is that a person with phobia should confront his fears by undertaking to experience something that will literally petrify him, like skydiving, bungee jumping, or riding a rollercoaster. The rationale for this theory is that the person will learn that the thing that stimulates his fears are actually not that dangerous and are reasonably safe, after experiencing such situations.

At present, ongoing research are still undertaken to search for the definite cause of acrophobia. Until such cause is found, it is imprudent to subject acrophobic to excessive heights without first treating the disorder.

6. Accept the disorder for what it is

This means that if your fear of heights interferes with your work or your daily life you should not try to endure it. You should accept that it is a real condition from which you suffer. Toughening up, by acting as if it does not exist or trying to deny it or hiding it from others, will only aggravate your situation. Denying its existence or concealing it would only further stress you, which in turn could lead you to make wrong decisions that might only endanger your life. You must learn to accept that having a phobia is nothing to be ashamed about and it is not a sign of weakness either that you need to conceal, especially if you are a man. Accept it for what it is, and you will fare better towards managing it and curing it.

Conclusion

Thank you again for purchasing this book!

I hope this book was able to help you to overcome your fear of heights.

Finally, if you enjoyed this book, then I'd like to ask you for a favor, would you be kind enough to leave a review for this book on Amazon? It'd be greatly appreciated!

Thank you and good luck!

Printed in Dunstable, United Kingdom